How To Write a Fiction Novel

How to Write a Book in 30 Days that is Sure To Be a Success

By Peter Kornfeld
Copyright © 2013

Income Disclaimer

This book contains business strategies, marketing methods and other business advice that, regardless of my own results and experience, may not produce the same results (or any results) for you. I make absolutely no guarantee, expressed or implied, that by following the advice below you will make any money or improve current profits, as there are several factors and variables that come into play regarding any given business.

Primarily, results will depend on the nature of the product or business model, the conditions of the marketplace, the experience of the individual, and situations and elements that are beyond your control.

As with any business endeavor, you assume all risk related to investment and money based on your own discretion and at your own potential expense.

Liability Disclaimer

By reading this book, you assume all risks associated with using the advice given below, with a full understanding that you, solely, are responsible for anything that may occur as a result of putting this information into action in any way, and regardless of your interpretation of the advice.

You further agree that our company cannot be held responsible in any way for the success or failure of your business as a result of the information presented in this book. It is your responsibility to conduct your own due diligence regarding the safe and successful operation of your business if you intend to apply any of our information in any way to your business operations.

Terms of Use

You are given a non-transferable, "personal use" license to this book. You cannot distribute it or share it with other individuals.

Also, there are no resale rights or private label rights granted when purchasing this book. In other words, it's for your own personal use only.

Table of Contents

How To Write a Fiction Novel

How to Write a Book in 30 Days that is Sure To Be a Success

By Peter Kornfeld

Introduction

Perhaps you've always had a good idea for a story and wanted to share it with the world. You may consider yourself to be an excellent storyteller, but just a bit unsure as to how to put it into writing. Though you may be in search of the best ways to bring a great idea to life, there are some simple but highly effective rules for writing a novel and making it work.

Sure if you happen to be a writer or somebody with excellent writing skills, then this can be easier than for others. The truth however lies in your ability to add depth to your book and that may be something that even the best writers have to work at.

A Different Mindset to Write a Novel Can Be Found By Anybody
Writing factual information is one thing, but bringing characters to life in a book that readers actually want to read is something entirely different. You may be surprised at just what it takes and once you get on a roll you can really develop an amazing story.

It's best to go with the philosophy that at the beginning there are absolutely no rules. Brainstorming is key throughout your ability to write a novel, but particularly at the start. Once you get to moving along you will find that the story sort of takes on a life of its own. You can then go back and "trim the fat" to create a story worth reading—and that readers simply can't put down!

This is a learned art and many writers spend their entire careers perfecting the art of writing a novel. It can however be done by the layperson with a great idea and a profound story to be told.

Though you may not realize it, you have the power to write a great novel, and you just might not realize it yet. So it's time to focus on the elements that create a great novel and then put emphasis on them as you move throughout your writing efforts.

So if you have that story that you are sure will create the perfect novel it's well worth a try. This is a totally different type of writing and creativity and imagination can really go a long way. The very best novels have characters, settings, and ideas that are deeply intriguing. At the end of it all you want a book that people can't stop turning the pages of, and you can accomplish that with the right attention to detail.

Here we will show you how to write a great novel and how to get your ideas out in a way that keeps others reading and you writing until the story is created and there for the world to take in. This is how you create a truly successful novel!

The ABC's of Story Telling

Though there is no "one size fits all" type formula for creating a good novel, there are a few guidelines that can really come in handy. You want to be sure that you keep the interests of the reader in mind as you develop a good storyline with interesting characters and the right amount of detail. In other words, you need to take the time to actually develop a story that will keep readers interested.

Certain Guidelines Always Hold True

Any good writer or one trying their hand at writing will tell you that there are some aspects of telling a story that hold true across the board. If you are trying to write a novel, no matter what the story line or the genre, you have to be sure that you maintain great focus on them. There are bound to be specifics that change with each story, but if you can maintain a good strong focus on these few elements then you will have great success.

Just as you like to hear people tell you a good story in person that they have put thought and details into, the same holds true for an actual book. It matters not if it's more of a romantic type of novel or an action packed drama, the point is that you have to be mindful of what the reader wants within a story. If you can put yourself into their mind frame then you will always create a winning storyline.

Think Like a Reader Would and You Can't Go Wrong

You want to be sure that you are always original, have winning ideas, and put something out there that you would want to read. Chances are if you have an interest in writing a novel it's because you are a bit of a reader yourself.

If that's the case then be sure to take keen interest in what people want to read and how you can get to that end result. If it's boring, duplicates what others have written, or drags on with no real point to it then your story is dead before it even begins!

So keep in mind the point of view of the reader, have fun with creating something truly interesting and fun, and above all ensure that you are always focused on the end product. If you can think of these rules then it will take shape as you move along, and that's a very good thing with this type of writing.

So What Are the Actual ABC's of Story Telling Anyhow?

There are three things that a good story should be. If you want to ensure that you gain readers and keep them, then you need to think through the real ABC's of storytelling to make your book a success. Some may come easy and some may require a bit more effort, but if you keep these at the forefront of your story development, then you simply can't go wrong.

- Authentic: Always above anything else be authentic and original in your ideas and your writing. Never go the route of copying somebody else's work, even if it's just for the concept. It's one thing to gather information by checking out others that you find interesting, but it's another to copy their work. Even "creative plagiarism" won't work for you because that shows through and it just appears to be duplicated. If you want to be taken seriously and want a story that really speaks to people, then by all means keep things original and ensure that you portray something that has never been done before.

- Bold: Make a statement, make an impact, make the characters, ideas, or plot pop off the page. If you want to ensure that people read your work then make it as bold as you can. Try to come up with new ways of telling a story and don't be afraid to be dramatic or even controversial. Though you may be afraid of pushing the limits, that's exactly what readers want you to do. There is a way to be classy and ensure it doesn't go above and beyond but also make it bold, so find that balance and work it.

- Captivating: It must be interesting, it must be compelling, and it must make a statement. Don't fall into the trap of being blah or boring and by all means make it a real page turner. If you think that something isn't interesting then it's not. If you think that something is outlandish then it very well may be, but that's what makes great stories. Make this as interesting and detailed as you possibly can and then you are sure to never disappoint—that's what gets readers to pick up your book and have a difficult time putting it down!

How to Brainstorm Well & Really Develop Your Story

Those who have experienced writing will tell you that brainstorming is the key to any good story. In this capacity it matters not what type of writing you are doing or for what kind of book as the basis is always the same. You want to be absolutely certain that you allow yourself some creative liberties at the beginning to really allow yourself to think and let the ideas flow uninterrupted.

Let the Ideas Flow and the Story Will Develop More Easily

This isn't always easy as we have a tendency to be hard on ourselves. We put an idea down on paper and then shoot ourselves down before it ever comes to life. We push ourselves hard to fully develop notions or ideas before they ever have a chance to unfold or develop. That's not how it works with writing and so you may have to adjust to a new mindset or way of thinking.

You see, brainstorming holds a very important part of story development. This is when you sit down with a pad of paper and a pen or whatever tool works best for you and just let the ideas flow. This may take place all in one sitting or it may take place over the course of several days where you write things down as you go along and always keep yourself prepared for the new ideas that come your way.

This is not a time to limit yourself and that's really important to remember here! As a general whole we tend to be so hard on ourselves and that makes it nearly impossible when it comes to story development. We will look at the ins and outs of developing a story, but for now suffice it to say that brainstorming is the key to your success.

It is what will keep you going strong and what will ensure that you create the basis of a book that readers will be interested in. Without brainstorming you are limited and that creativity just isn't showing through. The reader can pick up on that and therefore you must place great emphasis on the brainstorming to get you going and let the story unfold.

How Does Brainstorming Work and What Can It Do for You?

Whether you have been practicing brainstorming for a while or you are completely new at it, here are a few helpful guidelines to ensure that you get the most out of it for writing a novel.

- Don't ever limit yourself at the initial stages of brainstorming: When you first sit down to put pen to paper, let the ideas just flow. They don't need to make sense or tie together. They don't need to have a theme or characters or any sort of logic to them. The ideas are what you will use to move forward with creating the book and so you want them to be creative and off the cuff. If you limit yourself then you won't get everything that you can out of this stage and you just might miss out on something great.

- Let the ideas flow and jot down anything that you think of: As you are going through the creative brainstorming process, write down everything that you think of. Keep a pad of paper with you at all times and use this as the basis to let wonderful ideas come to life. So whether you are sitting in traffic, you just got up in the morning, or you are busy during your day, you always have a way of capturing the great ideas that you have. There is always an initial brainstorming session but this process can keep going for quite some time.

- Take the brainstorming ideas and try to compose them into a story one piece at a time: This happens only as you move forward so don't be in a rush for it. Try to look for complementary ideas and then combine them as much as possible. See where there are obvious connections and then make them with what you have in front of you. This may be a long process as you connect the dots or it may happen easily, but you will know and see when you are done with the brainstorming and ready for the story to begin to take shape.

- Be patient and let your story unfold, it all stems from good and uninterrupted brainstorming: Give yourself time and space to make this all come together. Be patient, take it in pieces, and just see

17

what transpires. You may find that you think up great ideas when you see what you already have and that's perfectly fine. Brainstorming doesn't just happen all at once for it can occur as you move forward with story development. This is the basis of a great story and it's slowly happening right before your very eyes!

The Necessity for a Premise & What Makes People Care About Your Story?

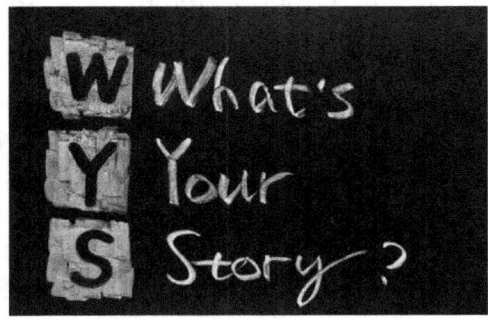

Though you may not have given it too much thought, there is a need for why your story exists. In your mind your story is a very important one to tell. For you the book you write will have meaning and perhaps its own story behind it. To the rest of the world however there must be a premise or else there is really no point in reading on. Harsh but true, a premise is the glue that holds the entire story together!

Reflect Upon Why People Would Want to Read Your Story

Essentially when you think of the premise it's why people should care about reading your book and that matters greatly if you wish to make your novel a success. This is where you get down to the nitty gritty and really dig deep as to what the reason for telling this story is. Think about it from your own point of view, would you read a book that had no point to it or reason for existence? Probably not!

The premise is essentially the guideline to the story, it helps to create a background and backbone behind the storyline. The story begins to come about because of this premise and so it is the starting point or the reason behind things. Without the premise, you have a lot of ideas that aren't very neatly bound together and that never makes sense in the end.

Your story may be within a certain genre, time period, or have a particular point of view to it. In the end it must be something that stands out from all others in its own unique way. Not only does this ensure that you aren't practicing plagiarism, but it also conveys the reason that you wrote the story to begin with.

If you can put yourself into the mindset of the reader that you hope to attract that can go a long way. If you can think through what a target reader is for your novel and then try to put together the premise based upon that, then it will really provide a great supportive role. You can sell novels if you put thought into the rationale for its existence.

If you can ask yourself why somebody should pick up your book, why they should care, and why they should ultimately buy it, then you are going to be in good shape as you move forward with your efforts.

Putting a Premise Into a Workable Viewpoint and Story Line

You have a story to tell and you want to share it with people. You want people to pick up your novel and know that this is something compelling that they simply must read. If you can think through that then you know and understand what a premise is all about, and here's how you get to that and why it matters.

- It's the "so what" of your story: Why do I as a reader care about your story? What makes this particular novel compelling or relevant? What is going to make me want to turn the pages and stay glued to the story line? Why does this story need to be told? These are all questions that you should be thinking through as you begin to develop your novel. After the brainstorming finishes, the premise and the entire reason for the book's existence comes into play and helps you to move forward.

- Think of what makes your story unique, special, or how it draws people in: There are likely plenty of books within your particular genre or that compare closely, and so you must think about what makes your book so important. What is special or unique about it? What is it about your book that will draw people in? It may be the storyline itself, the characters, or simply the voice that it's told within. There is however something that makes your book compelling, so think of that and use it to move you forward.

- Be mindful of considering the premise of the story along the way and work on perfecting it: After the brainstorming comes the reason for the book's true purpose and then you embrace this moving forward. After you think of the great ideas you need to think about how to put them together and why you are putting them together. If you can think through that and use this as your guideline moving forward then you have yourself a wonderful starting point—and this will keep you going all along the way if you always keep the premise at the core of your thoughts!

Allowing Your Story to Unfold & Adding Structure to Make It Work

There's a reason for your story and you've already thought of that, but now it's time to let your story unfold as you move forward. This is taking brainstorming to the next level. This is about integrating your premise and beginning to let the entire thing take shape. This is also where you begin to come up with unique points and interesting aspects of the story.

A Structure Creates a Perfect Beginning To Your Writing Efforts

There is a method to the madness and a way of going about this that can really make sense. Though you never want to limit yourself or cut yourself short in terms of creativity or writing skills, you do want to ensure that there is some sort of structure or backbone to the story as it moves forward. Without this you may lack a certain finesse or finished product that you are working towards.

This is taking the premise to the next level and really asking yourself what the point of the story is as you move forward. This is where you take all of the ideas that you have gathered from brainstorming and turning them into a well defined and interesting outline that you can work off of. This is ultimately a great way of getting organized so that you can then add the meat of the story to this great initial starting point!

Whereas in brainstorming, you never limit yourself and let the creative ideas keep flowing, this is the point at which you try to bring some order to those ideas. You take what you have jotted down and try to make some sense out of it. This is therefore the next natural step in the process and it is an essential one.

This doesn't mean that you have to clearly define each and every step in the novel now, but it does mean that you are going to have a strong working structure to which you create a meaningful story line off of. This is how you take creative ideas and turn them into a working structure that makes sense and that you can begin to fill out in terms of your ideas and story line. This is where things really start to come together and it can be quite exciting!

How Do You Make Sense Out Of This and Bring It All Together?

This step is going to take you some time because you may write down certain aspects of your structure and then go back and change it up a bit. You may find that you like how certain ideas flow and then decide that other areas need a bit of attention. Here are some helpful guidelines to ensure that you can move forward in a cohesive manner.

- Create a structure or outline first to help you put the ideas together: An outline always helps you to organize your thoughts, and this is no different. Consider this a sort of working "to do list" for your story. Taking the brainstorming and finding major areas of categorization or even chapters really works well. Recognize that it very well may change shape and be revamped several times over, but to get started an outline or working structure can be of great help in allowing you to organize your thoughts and make it work to your advantage.

- Add meat to the story as you go along but use the structure as your backbone: Once you have a working outline then you get to work on the meat of the story and let it really start to fill in. This is where you take a general concept or chapter of your story and begin to add the filler to it. This is where your story really begins to take shape and flow. It's not going to happen overnight and it will change shape several times over, but it is a good starting point. You went through the brainstorming process for a reason and this is where you allow things to come together and really enjoy the ex-citement as a story begins to slowly unfold.

- Always keep the premise in mind but let the ideas come together in a unique and cohesive way: As you move forward you don't want to beat yourself up in your thinking and creative writing, but you most certainly do want to keep your premise in mind. Keeping asking yourself why people care and keep taking note of what the point of your ideas really may be. If you can put yourself into that mindset and ensure the point of view of your reader, then the structure and the actual meat of the story will begin to be defined. This is very exciting when it occurs!

- Be sure that you don't limit yourself as you move forward and add in interesting points as they come to you: Do allow for a bit of creativity and a changing structure as you move along. Don't expect to stick to one working outline and be patient with yourself as it changes shape. This is only the beginning and though an important part of things, a true work in progress. Be patient, change things up as necessary, and use this organizational and creative process to your advantage—it will all come together as you move forward!

Discovering Your Setting & Making It Work

This may be the one element of a story that most people tend to forget—the setting of it all! Though this is an understandable mistake it can ensure that there is one element missing that makes your story a bit unclear in some instances. Though you may put careful detail into aspects of the story such as the premise and the characters, the setting can play a pivotal role as well.

The Setting Is The Entire Background of the Story Itself

The setting is what you can consider to be the backdrop or the background of the entire story itself. Sometimes it plays a rather pivotal role and sometimes it sort of blends in a bit behind the scenes. Even if the setting is not a major point to the story, you still must put some thought into it to make it work. This is a common mistake that many writers make as they believe it doesn't matter as much.

There are instances where the setting is going to play just as important of a role as the characters themselves. If you are writing a novel that is centered around a particular time period or if the setting really plays into the story such as a war peace or something where the character's actions are tied into where they dwell, then you are going to put great effort into it.

Even if the setting isn't as important as the other elements of the story, it helps to make the story real and tangible. If you set the reader up to understand what is going on in the background, where the characters live and what is happening in the background then it makes the story somehow seem more credible.

Think about what you would want out of a good story and chances are that you want to know some details of the character's life. The premise itself is based on a location, whether it's geographical in nature or even in a time period or at some particular place. You would want to know that level of detail and so does your reader.

Always keep in mind what you would center on when you read something and you can never go wrong! So if you hadn't given much thought to what is happening in the background, it's time to pay attention to this and include it within your thinking and writing process—here are some helpful tips to keep in mind as you do.

What Makes For a Good Setting and Why Does It Matter?

You have probably enjoyed a good book due in large part to setting. Even it's a less important detail, it's still something to put thought into. Here are some helpful guidelines to keep in mind as you flush out the setting of your novel.

- This is the background of your story that makes it all flow properly: You can have characters, you can have a premise, you can have a great storyline—but it doesn't all tie in well if you don't also have the setting as the backdrop. You can tell that something is missing, you can see that the characters want a place to somehow blend together. So the setting becomes quite important in tying every single detail together neatly!

- It can play a rather large role if it's set in a specific time period or if it plays into the genre specifically: If you are going for a very specific location, aspect of geography or part of the world, time period, or some other very detailed genre then the setting can be just as important as the characters themselves. You may or may not realize that and so as you brainstorm and then flush out the ideas, be certain to put in a lot of thought to what the setting is and how it plays out. Very specific details count and work quite well with this type of situation!

- You want to put some elaborate details in as it can really help your story come to life: One of the major differences between a good story and a great story is the level of detail that the writer puts in. You know that you've had a page turner before and it's because all of the details are so lively, so real, and so spelled out that you feel like you are there. You may not have lived through this time period personally but you understand what it's going to take to make it real for readers. You may need to do some research and really help to drive this aspect of the story so that it makes the story tangible and enjoyable for the reader. It really be-comes like an extension of real life!

How to Make Your Characters Pop Off the Pages & Really Sizzle

One of the lifelines of your story is undoubtedly the characters. These are what make your story so real and what the readers really get invested into. They begin to think of your characters as almost real life and they can place them into their own scenario. If you write the characters well then they are identifiable in the life of the reader and therefore pop off the page!

Think of What Each Character Is All About and Dive In From There

This is a very exciting notion, but it can also be quite overwhelming. There are some characters that seem to come to life without any problem. You get into writing a certain persona and just run with it. There are other characters that take a bit more to develop and therefore you need some extra time to make it all come to life. In any case you want to be sure to spend some extra time on this detail of things as it counts tremendously.

To write outstanding characters is to be reflective in nature. You want to think of what your story is really about or consider the premise. Think through the setting, the time period, or the backdrop of the story and then run with it from there. You may even lean on certain people or personalities that you have or have encountered in your own life and take bits and pieces from there.

Start by writing out who you want to be featured, or at least the type of person that you want to focus in on. If need be, then list out bullets and then let this all take the shape of the traits and personality that your characters will have. This is taking a human and almost breaking it apart so to speak.

You think of who the character is overall, what they stand for, what they are all about, what you like about them, what you find troubling about them, and develop the various aspects of them from there. This can be a very fun and rewarding element of writing a novel as you feel that you know these characters when it's all said and done!

Though it may take a significant amount of time and effort, your characters are what people will really sink their teeth into. If you write these characters well they will be what causes readers to happily turn the pages and to see what unfolds with the story of these people.

What Makes for Great Characters?
You've read that book where the characters are just amazing, so what makes them that way? You may even reflect back on certain characters well after you finish the book so how do you accomplish that in your own novel?

Here are some helpful tips to keep in mind to make these intriguing and captivating characters.

- Think of the types of characters that are really going to add pizzazz to your story: What gets you interested and drawn into a story? What type of person do you love or love to hate? Think of the types of characters that make for a truly intriguing element and then run with it. It's all about pizzazz and finesse and then just letting the character take on its own persona. This may come easily or it may take a bit of extra effort from you, but you will know when the characters are real life extensions of the story—and that's when it all sings for you!

- Use exaggeration and really push the traits of the characters to the limits: This is not a time to put in minimal effort or details, you want to really exaggerate everything quite extensively. The more detail, the more outrageousness, the more elaborate, and the more captivating, the better!

  Push the limits, really focus in on small minute little details of the personality. If they are funny use examples. If they are beautiful use descriptive words to convey just how gorgeous and why. Take it to a whole new level with the amount of detail and exaggeration that you place forth.

  Though you may think it's too much, it's never enough when it comes to this aspect of storytelling. What makes certain characters great is the fact that they are amped up versions of real life people that we know, and we hold nothing back in-

to writing about them and developing them. It really works!

- Think of what you find interesting in a story and
  then take it up a notch: What has made you turn
  the pages of a favorite book? What characters do
  you love to sink your teeth into? Even if they are
  not in the same genre or if they share a different
  level of detail, use your favorites as a starting
  point. Even if it's somebody that you love to hate
  or somebody absolutely repulsive that you have
  encountered in your own life, use that as a basis.
  This really creates an outstanding platform off of
  which to develop characters that sell the story and
  create the storyline for you one scenario or problem at a time.

- Really concentrate on all of the fine and specific
  details of the story so that they seem real and re-
  latable: This is all about fine tuning and getting into
  the nitty gritty because it really works. If you can
  get in touch with the very specific aspects of what
  each character is about then it all starts to take
  shape. Out of this thought process you may even
  very well find some supporting characters that you
  never even knew existed. You may find that you
  have these characters or the basis of them deep
  within you and you never even realized it. So for
  now be sure to let the character take control over
  the story, let them develop as you write, and really
  focus in on all of the best and most specific details
  of what makes them who they are. This is what
  makes for amazing and truly captivating charac-

ters that add that extra zing to a story—your readers will be in awe!

Hero vs. Villain and the Necessity of the Relationship

It's that notorious part of a book that makes it so very intriguing. It's the relationship that we may have in our own lives and struggle with, but we rather love to read about. It's an expanded version of the feelings that we have for somebody we consider to be evil. That relationship between hero and villain in a novel is what makes for some of the best detail!

Reflect on Good Vs. Evil Throughout Your Life
Though you may think that you are not capable of flexing your writing muscles to the extent necessary to make for good reading, you have more within you than you likely realize. In most instances we carry within us feelings and experiences of good vs. evil that can help to shape an

amazing storyline. This is what can contribute to amazing details of a great story that simply needs to be told, and we all have sentiments that can filter into this part of the process.

More than likely in your own life you have been both the hero and the villain. Every time you have seen the good vs. evil and related people play out in real life, you have yourself the makings of a good storyline. For this aspect of the story you want to reach within you and dig deep to get into the framework of the very best characters and plots within this realm. It exists within you, but you just might have to dig deep to get to it!

There are always experiences in life where we have seen the hero and the villain at work, and good vs. bad play out. It's reflecting upon those that helps us to embrace this writing opportunity and create something lasting and memorable out of it. Get in touch with the pain or the sentiments that accompanied those experiences and use that to power you through this aspect of writing.

The heroes and the villains are what makes a good story great. They expand upon just any other character and show emotion, definition, and even struggles that we can all identify with. You do want to be certain to really amp up the detail here and make the heroes truly amazing, and the villains of course deliciously terrible and diabolical in their own way. This is the type of storytelling that helps to make your novel truly amazing and the words leap right off the pages into everyday life!

What Makes the Hero Vs. Villain Such An Important Part of the Story Line?

It may seem obvious or it may be something that you have to really search for, but at the end of the day there is a great necessity for the hero vs. villain aspect of the story. If you are wondering why this is, here are some reasons to consider as you write:

- There has to be somebody that saves the day: We all want to believe that good always prevails and this is a perfect instance of that. We all want to see that somebody can rise above all challenges and life situations to save the day so to speak. We all must see this person play out in a book and understand that the hero will win out in the end, as it helps to boost our spirits. Therefore we need that hero to exist and to be somebody that we would personally look to.

  There is great importance behind a hero as they not only contribute to the story and ultimately save the day, but they also show us that good does exist in the world. We want to root for somebody and we want to see that good traits in life really do help to get you ahead. We must see this play out in a novel and so you must spend some time in developing the hero character as they will end up being a major focal point to the story. This aspect of the story is what may sell it to people in the long run!

- There must be that character that everybody loves to hate: Even if you have experienced villains or bullies in your own life and had your own terrible experiences with them, you want and need to see that this is part of a good story. We love to hate the bad guy and we want to see them struggle in the end. Secretly we all want to share some sort of characteristic of the bad guy because it's way more fun to be evil than to always be good. We must see this play out in the book and therefore as much as we think it's not a necessity, there must be a villain to play against the hero.

Every good story has some dark twist or turn or negative chain of events and the villain must be closely linked to that. So think through the terrible characteristics of a villain you have seen in your life and then use that to power you through and write this defined detail of a pivotal part of the story line and character development.

- The very struggle between good vs. evil is what people can sink their teeth into: Sometimes the best story lines are the struggle between good vs. evil and we all love to see this story play out. It's what our lives are built upon and therefore we must find a way to use this as a foundation for our novel.

  We want to see the good hero fall and the bad villain take over, at least temporarily. We want to hate the villain and all the evil that he stands for. We ultimately want to see the hero win out because we want to believe that's the way it works in real life. This struggle and story line that develops out of it is an absolute necessity and one that we must put good thought into.

- It may be more subtle or indirect but these characters and the relationship must be present: Even if your story is more specific in other areas, this part of the story line must be present. The good vs. evil may be more indirect or subtle but it must be there. Even if the hero is a little good or the villain isn't quite so evil, there must be some aspect of this that is present and worthwhile in the story.

So think through how you can incorporate the good vs. bad evolution and how you can create characters that even somehow match up to what you would expect as a result of it. This is really a fun part of the story to write, so even if it's indirect, make this come to life and make your novel a real page turner!

Creating Conflict and Using This as the Number One Rule Throughout

There are certain elements to what makes a good novel that we may not really embrace or care for in our own lives. One such element is that of conflict, which while it makes a good story is nothing that we like to deal with as we move throughout our lives. It is those uncomfortable feelings and frustration that we have all dealt with that help to shape a good storyline and to make it compelling for all to read.

Conflict Is a Reality and a Necessary Part of a Good Novel

The reality is that conflict exists in everyday life, and though we may not like it in our dealings it is always going to be there. You would have no real story or ups and downs without a conflict and so the necessity of it contributing to a good storyline is inevitable. You may even find a bit of inspiration through your own struggles to help find what conflict the characters of your book may face.

Out of the situations that are difficult comes the ability to rise above. Out of the best scenarios comes an appreciation for them when everything goes wrong. Every story, whether fiction or true life, has a turning point and a place where things change over. It is that very moment that we must embrace and how we define a good story that our novel centers around.

The conflict is a major component to our storyline. It may tie into the premise or may help to define characters and the reason for their being. It may show how the strong rise above and the weak fall. It shows that even the most heroic characters struggle in some way and have their very fiber tested. This is a true testament to the way that things are in real life and why a conflict must exist within every good novel.

If everything went along problem free in real life it would be nice, but it would also be boring. We all have problems and challenges in our real life and so they must be present in a good book. Problem free living does not make for good reading!

So if you want to adapt a storyline that others will read and follow along with, then conflict must be part of it. Not only does this make for good reading, but it also makes for a realistic depiction of the way that things are. We must portray this and ensure that our characters have a way of dealing with whatever comes their way—just like real life!

Conflict Is The Life Blood of a Good Story
Without conflict you are missing a major element of a story line. Therefore we absolutely must be sure that it is present and portrayed properly to pull everything together. Here are some important guidelines to remember when it comes to conflict in our novels.

- There must always be a turning point: You can sometimes foresee when the turning point is coming and sometimes you are surprised when it hits you. There is however a necessity for things to turn over from good to bad. This is where we see a character's strength tested and when we can really sink our teeth into a story line. You want a good build up to get to the turning point and then a way of moving things along when it seems that bad will prevail over everything.

- There must always be some sort of struggle or conflict to keep the story interesting: The hero must struggle with their identity, it must appear that the villain or evil will win out over all, or there must be something that puts the entire story line or happiness in jeopardy. It's not that we benefit from other people's struggles but we absolutely must find a way to see that though conflict comes about, there are surefire ways to overcome it all and move forward.

- Keeping things happy go lucky will not make for a selling novel—there must be something that goes wrong at some point: Think of it quite simply— conflict makes for a good story and a lack of it does not! If you want people to really embrace your story and get interested and involved in it, then you must present some sort of conflict within the story line. You want people to feel invested in what happens to the characters and how the story turns around when bad things happen. If every-

45

thing went along well without any hiccups then ultimately that's boring! If we're really honest about
it, that's boring even in real life. So though we may
not love to deal with actual conflicts, we recognize
the importance of them within a story line and
therefore must put great effort into bringing it out in
our own novel.

Rising to the Climax And Making Drama Work for You In Your Writing

You know that moment when you read a book or even see a movie and you can just feel the build up? That's the climax at work and an essential element of just about every storyline. It is truly a necessity and something that you must invest time and effort into, to make your story work. This is an aspect of drama and it helps to define it in an entirely new way.

Every Story Must Have an Element of Drama and a Climax

It matters not what sort of genre your book is in. It doesn't matter as much what types of characters you feature, what your story line is all about, or what time period your story takes place in—for within every story line must come some sort of drama and of course a climax to the story! Without this it automatically feels as though something is missing and so you can understand firsthand how it all works.

It's that build up that gets readers intrigued and truly invested in your story. It's that sort of emotional investment that gets them to really react and relate to what you put together. Without a climax the story can tend to fall flat and so you see and understand the true necessity of it.

This may be an area that you struggle with, but if you put in the right amount of thought you can make it work. Begin by thinking of the absolute worst circumstances that could happen to your characters or the storyline and then move from there. This is about putting forth some terrible turning point and building up to it so that you can feel this as you read it. You may even be able to see the climax and build up actually occurring and from there it's all in how you solve it or make things work beyond this pivotal point.

You want readers to feel like they are on the edge of their seat as they work to figure out what will happen next. The climax or the element of drama may be a bit more subtle or it may be more pressing, but the point is that it is there and present. You want to be sure that you spend some great thought on figuring out what sort of circumstances will present themselves so that the building up of the story takes on a life of its own.

This takes time, talent, and a concerted effort to create. It's essential that every good novel has some sort of problem to solve or unimaginable circumstance to deal with. Though you certainly wouldn't want to deal with these things in your own life, they help to shape and mold a good story and help to make it captivating for the readers. Drama in the end can add so much to your novel!

Drama and a Good Climax Can Add Greatly To Your Story Line

Drama may be an element of our own lives that we don't like to deal with, but it always has a place in a good novel. If you want to captivate your readers and draw them in, then you need to have a good build up, some sort of drama, and of course a way for it all to unfold in an exciting way. Here's how it all ties in together:

- You need build up and intense emotional reaction: You want your readers to react emotionally to what you have written. It may not always be in a positive way as a true climax really tests the characters and their boundaries. You want them to feel disgust for the villain and empathy for the hero and what they are going through. You also want this drama to build up throughout the book.

  It may start subtly but as you get towards the climax or the turning point of the story, you start to see how truly revolutionary and necessary this aspect of the story is. You want to build up until you reach the climax of the story and then spend the next part of the novel letting the characters pick up the pieces and figure out how to move forward with their lives. It's all about a good comeback!

- You need to have a way of getting readers on the edge of their seats: No matter what the premise of your story is or how it all unfolds, you want and need your readers to be drawn in. Ideally with the element of drama present and with a well built up climax, you start to see the readers become engaged early on. You want to be sure to grab their attention early on and keep them reading so that they can barely put the book down.

49

When you accomplish that point of the story where readers are literally and figuratively on the edge of their seats is when great things really start to happen. That's when you have reached true success in your storytelling and your ability to bring the premise of your story to life in a truly provocative way.

- You need to turn things around, but in a dramatic and therefore effective way: You set up the climax through the way in which you build up. You then must find a way to turn things around in a dramatic but collected way. If you can get in touch with that problem solving that makes for a happy ending, then you have achieved great success. Though it may not be all rainbows and big smiles, you do need to find a way to work towards some sort of closure at the end.

  This is where your ability to draw a climax and then move past it really becomes pivotal to the story itself. It may be more subtle or even unsettling but in some capacity you allow for the climax to be where things reach their peak or worse and then you work past it with the help and effort of a good ending that takes place. It all ties together and drama helps it to unfold in a truly interesting way, far and above what really happens in everyday life!

- You must be dramatic and insert great details about it along the way: You may not be a dramatic person by nature, but you must find a way to portray it within your novel. It may be a simple but well founded exaggeration of details or magnifying certain problems or elements of the story line. It may be that you put forth more problems or challenges for the typical hero than may exist in real life.

It's all about finding that balance however and when you do then it makes for a story line that is compelling to the average reader. We may not want excessive drama in real life but we certainly want it in a good story, and so the more well expressed drama you can portray the better off your story will be in the end!

Go Back and Cut the Fat to Create a Book That Readers Keep Wanting to Read

When you first start out with writing a book it's all about brainstorming and working to come up with as many ideas as possible. As you move forward you tend to widdle it down but also want to be sure to write down the ideas that come to mind. This makes for a nice balance and a great way of telling a story. When you get to the end of it all, then it's all about cutting back a bit and ensuring that you have a well polished final product.

Editing Plus Final Writing Makes for a Necessary and Fruitful End to the Book

This may be the toughest part of the book writing process because now you are truly in editing mode. Sure you are still doing some writing, but in the end it's all about getting rid of any duplication and ensuring that there is a good flow and nice balance with the book that you put out. So when you reach the end stage of writing a novel, it's all about trimming the fat so to speak.

This can be a bit challenging as you may initially think that all of your ideas are valuable. It's not to say that they aren't, but you again have to put yourself into the mindset of the reader. What are they going to care about? What is really going to matter to them in terms of the story itself and the details that you put into it? If something doesn't seem to add value or seems like unnecessary detail or duplication, then it's well worth getting rid of.

You want to find a nice middle ground where it's not too much detail but not lacking in it either. Too much of a good thing can be overwhelming and can make the reader feel lost or even bored—that's never a good thing! Too little of a good thing makes them feel as if they didn't get enough out of the story and therefore they are wanting more. The end result is that they won't be interested or recommend your book. It is your job as the writer to find that balance and to make it all work together!

So this stage may seem like an awful lot of work but it's going to go a long way. The detail that you put forth is going to really ensure that you end up with something polished and well put together. So spend the time now to trim the fat and get to the heart of the story. If you do then it will show and that's what draws readers in and makes them want to keep coming back for more!

Getting To the Important Stuff Really Does Count

So if you feel lost as to what to cut out and what to keep, you are not alone. That sentiment is shared by just about every reader that wants to put together an amazing story. Here we look at a few ways to trim the fat and stick with the really important stuff to create a story that works tremendously.

- Be sure to read through everything again and cut back as necessary: The very best writers read through their material again and again. This is an essential step to ensure great success with your book and should therefore be an automatic part of your process. Though this may seem cumbersome you want to be certain that all grammar and verbiage is properly written. By reading through again you are also sure to find some ideas that can be cut back or eliminated altogether.

  This is an essential part of editing and something that you should do without thought. You need to read through what you've written anyhow, so doing it along the way and then again at the end can prove to be quite helpful. Then you know that you are on top of everything and what you end up with is writing perfection!

- Portray your ideas with great detail, but get rid of anything that is repetitive in nature: You have hopefully included a great amount of specifics and detail within your writing. You have likely embellished with even the tiniest part of things and really made the story and the characters jump off the pages.

  Now it's time to do a run through to see which ideas are covered properly and which are a bit repetitive in nature. You want a lot of great detail but you don't want the story to get lost within this. It's helpful to cut out anything that is repetitive or that deters from the story—never let the reader get bogged down in so much detail that it can become frustrating or overwhelming. That's an instant turn off!

- Trim any fat or unnecessary aspects of the story to keep it interesting: We all know that when we write we may be deep in thought as we do so. It is now time to see which aspects of the writing and the story are unnecessary in nature, and which must stay. This is tough as you don't want to lose the essence of the story or remove an important detail, but it has to be done.

  Here you are going to review what you have written and decide which areas are ultimately fat so to speak. If you have too much flowery language, far too much repetition, or even have details that really aren't that important then that's when it's time to cut back. It may be tough at first but you will get on a roll and also learn to be keener to this as you move forward. This comes with experience and you'll be amazed at how well you develop this skill.

- Always think through what a reader is going to want to see out of your story and adapt to that mindset: Again it's time to put yourself into the mindset of the reader. You want to be sure that they can understand what you are trying to say and that you have created a truly good story.

  Beyond that it's all about thinking through what they will care about and what they won't. They want characters that really speak to them and a unique storyline and premise. Beyond that however it's all about thinking like the person that you are trying to reach out to with your story. That's a helpful rule of thumb to help with editing and writing as well.

- Put out a good story that focuses on only the relevant aspects of the story: You want to find the best balance in this area. Within the pertinent aspects of the story you want the details to be outstanding and truly revolutionary to the story. For the deeper details you need to ask yourself if they really do matter or if they are simply a waste of time. This is for you as the writer to decide and it may take a couple of read throughs.

Don't beat yourself up if you can't think of what details remain and what go after just one review, as it often takes a bit more time and focus. So think about what supports the story or sets up a character and then focus on that, all the while getting rid of what you find to be noise or clutter within the big picture of the story. This is a good rule of thumb to help you get focused and edit your work properly.

Conclusion

Writing a novel is a lot of work, but if you have the ideas in your head and the motivation then it's something that you should absolutely move forward with. This is a great venture to take on and if you focus on these specific areas then you will find that it's not just for a professional writer. You can write a novel if you stay focused, bring your great story to life, and pay close attention to the various aspects of what makes a great book.

It may seem like a daunting task at first, but with the right focus you can absolutely turn a great idea or story line into a novel that readers will enjoy. This takes time, dedication, and a great initial brainstorming session. Though you are sure to cut back on some of your ideas as you move forward and go to edit mode, at the beginning it's all about coming up with as many great ideas as you can—so enjoy this creative part of the process!

You want great characters both good and bad that people can really sink their teeth into. You want to see the story of good vs. evil unfold before you and ensure that the readers will be in awe of what you bring out in the pages of the novel. You need to always try to think like your reader to ensure that what you create is something that they will enjoy and recommend to their friends.

The guidelines presented to you can help you to organize your thoughts and focus on the things that really matter to your readers. This is what will take a great idea and turn it into a really captivating story. You can really help to develop a premise, a story line, and characters that people will enjoy reading about and that's what sells novels. So now you have the framework of what makes for a really intriguing novel that is sure to be a success, the rest is up to you to develop.

Happy writing and best of luck with your novel!